THE DESSERT COOKBOOK FOR BEGINNERS

100 unique and easy-to-make recipes to Satisfy Your Craving

Emily lee

All rights reserved.

Disclaimer

The information contained in this eBook is meant to serve as a comprehensive collection of strategies that the author of this eBook has done research about. Summaries, strategies, tips, and tricks are only recommendations by the author, and reading this eBook will not guarantee that one's results will exactly mirror the author's results. The author of the eBook has made all reasonable efforts to provide current and accurate information for the readers of the eBook. The author and its associates will not be held liable for any unintentional error or omissions that may be found. The material in the eBook may include information by third parties. Third-party materials comprise opinions expressed by their owners. As such, the author of the eBook does not assume responsibility or liability for any third-party material or opinions. Whether because of the progression of the internet, or the unforeseen changes in company policy and editorial submission guidelines, what is stated as fact at the time of this writing may become outdated or inapplicable later.

The eBook is copyright © 2022 with all rights reserved. It is illegal to redistribute, copy, or create derivative work from this eBook whole or in part. No parts of this report may be reproduced or retransmitted in any reproduced or retransmitted in any forms whatsoever without the writing expressed and signed permission from the author.

TABLE OF CONTENTS

TABLE OF CONTENTS 3
INTRODUCTION 7
1. ITALIAN ARTICHOKE PIE 8
2. SPAGHETTI MEATBALL PIE 11
3. CHOCOLATE PANNA COTTA 14
4. CHEESY GALETTE WITH SALAMI 16
5. PANNA COTTA 19
6. CARAMEL FLAN 21
7. CATALAN CREAM 23
8. ORANGE-LEMON SPANISH CREAM 26
9. DRUNKEN MELON 28
10. ALMOND SORBET 30
11. SPANISH APPLE TORTE 32
12. CARAMEL CUSTARD 35
13. SPANISH CHEESECAKE 37
14. SPANISH FRIED CUSTARD 40
15. ITALIAN BAKED PEACHES 43
16. SPICY ITALIAN PRUNE-PLUM CAKE 45
17. SPANISH NUT CANDY 48
18. HONEYED PUDDING 50
19. SPANISH ONION TORTE 53
20. SPANISH PAN SOUFFLÉ 56
21. FROZEN HONEY SEMIFREDDO 58
22. CILANTRO INFUSED AVOCADO LIME SORBET 61
23. PUMPKIN PIE CHEESECAKE 63
24. MOCHA ICE CREAM 66
25. CHERRY AND CHOCOLATE DONUTS 68
26. BLACKBERRY PUDDING 71
27. PUMPKIN PIE WITH MAPLE SYRUP 73
28. RUSTIC COTTAGE PIE 75

29.	CHOCOLATE AMARETTO FONDUE	78
30.	FLANS WITH A RASPBERRY COULIS	80
31.	FRUIT BALLS IN BOURBON	83
32.	PECAN PIE ICE CREAM	85
33.	CINNAMON CHIP BREAD PUDDING	88
34.	BAKED CARAMEL APPLES	91
35.	GIVE THANKS PUMPKIN PIE	94
36.	LOW FAT PUMPKIN TRIFLE	96
37.	PUMPKIN DUMP CAKE	99
38.	CHIA PUDDING	101
39.	APPLE TREATS	103
40.	BUTTERNUT SQUASH MOUSSE	105
41.	SOUTHERN SWEET POTATO PIE	107
42.	SWEET POTATO AND COFFEE BROWNIES	110
43.	THANKSGIVING CORN SOUFFLÉ	113
44.	CRANBERRY ICE CREAM	115
45.	WALNUT PETITES	118
46.	THANKSGIVING CARROT SOUFFLÉ	121
47.	PUMPKIN FLAN	123
48.	COUNTRY CORN CASSEROLE	127
49.	CRANBERRY PECAN RELISH	129
50.	TURKEY AND POTATO HASH CAKES	131
51.	APPLE CRUNCH COBBLER	134
52.	GOOEY AMISH CARAMEL PIE	137
53.	AUTUMN LEAVES	140
54.	HARVEST FRUIT COMPOTE	142
55.	THANKSGIVING CRANBERRY PIE	144
56.	SPARKLING CRANBERRIES	147
57.	TORTE WITH LEMON FILLING	149
58.	CHOCOLATE AMARETTO FONDUE	152
59.	FLANS WITH A RASPBERRY COULIS	154
60.	CHOCOLATE CAKE	157
61.	FLAN ALMENDRA	160

62.	Spiced strawberries	163
63.	Blackberry fool	165
64.	Zabaglione	167
65.	Raspberries and cream	169
66.	Fruit balls in bourbon	171
67.	Indian-style mangoes	173
68.	Italian cheesecake	175
69.	Lemon fluff	177
70.	Almond and coconut meringues	179
71.	Chocolate Chip Cookies	181
72.	Air Fryer Brownies	183
73.	Berry Cheesecake	186
74.	Donuts in the Air Fryer	189
75.	Vanilla Strawberry Cream Cake	192
76.	Berry Cobbler	195
77.	Chocolate Bundt Cake	197
78.	Giant PB Cookie	200
79.	Dessert Bagels	202
80.	Bread Pudding	204
81.	Mini Strawberry and Cream Pies	206
82.	Brazilian Grilled Pineapple	208
83.	Coconut Crusted Cinnamon Bananas	210
84.	Gluten Free Easy Coconut Pie	213
85.	Pecan Pudding	215
86.	Coffee Liqueur Mousse	217
87.	Peach Melba Dessert	219
88.	Frozen Cinnamon Nut Yogurt	221
89.	Five-minute fudge	223
90.	Almond-Oat Crust	225
91.	Apple Fantasy Dessert	227
92.	Avocado ice cream	229
93.	Banana Cream Pie	231
94.	Berry Fool	233

95.	Berry Tiramisu	235
96.	Butter Rum Caramels	238
97.	Candied Citrus Peel	240
98.	Cardamom-Coconut Panna Cotta	242
99.	Chicory Cream Brulee	245
100.	Mint Chocolate Fondue	247

CONCLUSION 249

INTRODUCTION

Dessert is a course that concludes a meal. The course consists of sweet foods, such as confections, and possibly a beverage such as dessert wine and liqueur. In some parts of the world, such as much of Central Africa and West Africa, and most parts of China, there is no tradition of a dessert course to conclude a meal.

The term dessert can apply to many confections, such as biscuits, cakes, cookies, custards, gelatins, ice creams, pastries, pies, puddings, macaroons, sweet soups, tarts, and fruit salad. Fruit is also commonly found in dessert courses because of its naturally occurring sweetness. Some cultures sweeten foods that are more commonly savory to create desserts.

1. Italian artichoke pie

Servings: 8 Servings

Ingredient

- 3 Eggs; Beaten
- 1 3 Oz Package Cream Cheese with Chives; Softened
- ¾ teaspoon Garlic Powder
- ¼ teaspoon Pepper
- 1½ cup Mozzarella Cheese, Part Skim Milk; Shredded
- 1 cup Ricotta Cheese
- ½ cup Mayonnaise
- 1 14 Oz Can Artichoke Hearts; Drained
- ½ 15 Oz Can Garbanzo Beans, Canned; Rinsed and Drained
- 1 2 1/4 Oz Can Sliced Olives; Drained
- 1 2 Oz Jar Pimientos; Diced and Drained
- 2 tablespoons Parsley; Snipped
- 1 Pie Crust (9 Inch); Unbaked
- 2 smalls Tomato; Sliced

Directions:

a) Combine eggs, cream cheese, garlic powder, and pepper in a large mixing basin. Combine 1 cup mozzarella cheese, ricotta cheese, and mayonnaise in a mixing bowl.

b) Stir until everything is well blended.

c) Cut 2 artichoke hearts in half and set aside. Chop the rest of the hearts.

d) Toss the cheese mixture with the chopped hearts, garbanzo beans, olives, pimientos, and parsley. Fill the pastry shell with the mixture.

e) Bake for 30 minutes at 350 degrees. The remaining mozzarella cheese and Parmesan cheese should be sprinkled on top.

f) Bake for another 15 minutes or until set.

g) Leave to rest for 10 minutes.

h) Over the top, arrange tomato slices and quartered artichoke hearts.

i) Serve

2. Spaghetti meatball pie

Servings: 4-6

Ingredients:

- 1 - 26 oz. bag of beef Meatballs
- 1/4 cup chopped green pepper
- 1/2 cup chopped onion
- 1 - 8 oz. package spaghetti
- 2 eggs, slightly beaten
- 1/2 cup grated Parmesan cheese
- 1-1/4 cups shredded mozzarella cheese
- 26 oz. jar chunky spaghetti sauce

Directions:

a) Preheat oven to 375°F. Sauté peppers and onions until softened, about 10 minutes. Set aside.

b) Cook spaghetti, drain and rinse with cold water and pat dry. Place in large mixing bowl.

c) Add eggs and Parmesan cheese and stir to combine. Press mixture into the bottom of a sprayed 9" pie plate. Top with 3/4 cup shredded mozzarella cheese. Thaw frozen meatballs in microwave for 2 minutes.

d) Cut each meatball in half. Layer the meatball halves over the cheese mixture. Combine spaghetti sauce with cooked peppers and onions.

e) Spoon over meatball layer. Loosely cover with foil and bake for 20 minutes.

f) Remove from oven and sprinkle 1/2 cup mozzarella cheese over the spaghetti sauce mixture.

g) Continue to bake uncovered for another 10 minutes until bubbly. Cut into wedges and serve.

3. Chocolate Panna Cotta

5 portions

Ingredients:

- 500 ml heavy cream
- 10 g gelatin
- 70 g black chocolate
- 2 tablespoon of yogurt
- 3 tablespoon of sugar
- a pinch of salt

Directions:

a) In a small amount of cream, soak gelatine.

b) In a small saucepan, pour the remaining cream. Bring the sugar and yogurt to a boil, stirring occasionally, but do not boil. Remove the pan from the heat.

c) Stir in the chocolate and gelatine until they are completely dissolved.

d) Fill the molds with the batter and chill for 2-3 hours.

e) To release the panna cotta from the mold, run it under hot water for a few seconds before removing the dessert.

f) Decorate to your liking and serve!

4. Cheesy Galette with Salami

5 portions

Ingredients:

- 130 g butter
- 300 g flour
- 1 teaspoon salt
- 1 egg
- 80 ml milk
- 1/2 teaspoon vinegar
- Filling:
- 1 tomato
- 1 sweet pepper
- zucchini
- salami
- mozzarella
- 1 Tablespoon olive oil
- herbs (such as thyme, basil, spinach)

Directions:

a) Cube up the butter.

b) In a bowl or pan, combine the oil, flour, and salt and chop with a knife.

c) Toss in an egg, some vinegar, and some milk.

d) Begin kneading the dough. Refrigerate for half an hour after rolling it into a ball and wrapping it in plastic wrap.

e) Cut all of the filling Ingredients.

f) Place the filling in the center of a large circle of dough that has been rolled out on baking parchment (except Mozzarella).

g) Drizzle with olive oil and season with salt and pepper.

h) Then carefully lift the dough's edges, wrap them around the overlapping sections, and lightly press them in.

i) Preheat oven to 200°C and bake for 35 minutes. Add the mozzarella ten minutes before the end of the baking time and continue to bake.

j) Serve immediately!

5. Panna Cotta

Servings: 6

Ingredients:

- ⅓ cup milk
- 1 packet unflavored gelatin
- 2 ½ cups heavy cream
- ¼ cup sugar
- ¾ cup sliced strawberries
- 3 Tablespoons brown sugar
- 3 Tablespoons brandy

Directions:

a) Stir the milk and gelatin together until the gelatin is completely dissolved. Remove from the equation.

b) In a small saucepan, bring the heavy cream and sugar to a boil.

c) Incorporate the gelatin mixture into the heavy cream and whisk for 1 minute.

d) Divide the mixture among 5 ramekins.

e) Place plastic wrap over the ramekins. After that, chill for 6 hours.

f) In a mixing bowl, combine the strawberries, brown sugar, and brandy; chill for at least 1 hour.

g) Place the strawberries on top of the panna cotta.

6. Caramel Flan

Servings: 4

Ingredients:

- 1 Tablespoons vanilla extract
- 4 eggs
- 2 cans milk (1 evaporated and 1 sweetened condensed)
- 2 cups whipping cream
- 8 Tablespoons sugar

Directions:

a) Preheat the oven to 350 degrees Fahrenheit.

b) In a nonstick pan, melt sugar over medium heat until golden.

c) Pour the liquefied sugar into a baking pan while it is still hot.

d) In a mixing dish, crack and beat eggs. Combine the condensed milk, vanilla extract, cream, and sweetened milk in a mixing bowl. Make a thorough mix.

e) Pour the batter into the melted sugar-coated baking pan. Place the pan in a larger pan with 1 inch of boiling water.

f) Bake for 60 minutes.

7. Catalan Cream

Servings: 3

Ingredients:

- 4 egg yolks
- 1 cinnamon (stick)
- 1 lemon (zest)
- 2 Tablespoons cornstarch
- 1 cup sugar
- 2 cups milk
- 3 cups Fresh Fruits (berries or figs)

Directions:

a) In a pan, whisk together egg yolks and a big portion of the sugar. Blend until the mixture is foamy and smooth.

b) Add the cinnamon stick with lemon zest. Make a thorough mix.

c) Mix in the cornstarch and milk. Under low heat, stir until the mixture thickens.

d) Take the pot out of the oven. Allow to cool for a few minutes.

e) Place the mixture in ramekins and set aside.

f) Set aside for at least 3 hours in the refrigerator.

g) When ready to serve, drizzle the remaining sugar over the ramekins.

h) Place the ramekins on the bottom shelf of the boiler. Allow the sugar to melt until it turns a golden brown color.

i) As a garnish, serve with fruits.

8. Orange-lemon Spanish cream

Servings: 1 Servings

Ingredient

- 4½ teaspoon Plain gelatin
- ½ cup Orange juice
- ¼ cup Lemon juice
- 2 cups Milk
- 3 Eggs, separated
- ⅔ cup Sugar
- Pinch of salt
- 1 tablespoon Grated orange rind

Directions:

a) Mix gelatin, orange juice, and lemon juice together and let aside for 5 minutes.

b) Scald the milk and whisk in the yolks, sugar, salt, and orange rind.

c) Cook in a double boiler until it coats the back of a spoon.

d) After that, add the gelatin mixture. Cool.

e) Add stiffly beaten egg whites into the mixture.

f) Refrigerate till set.

9. Drunken melon

Servings: 4 to 6 servings

Ingredient

- For the dish A selection of 3 to 6 different Spanish cheeses
- 1 Bottle port wine
- 1 Melon, top removed and deseeded

Directions:

a) One to three days before the supper, pour the port into the melon.

b) Chill in the refrigerator, covered in plastic wrap and with the top replaced.

c) Remove the melon from the refrigerator and remove the wrap and top when ready to serve.

d) Remove the port from the melon and place it in a bowl.

e) Cut the melon into pieces after removing the rind. Place the pieces in four separate chilled dishes.

f) Serve on a side dish with the cheeses.

10. Almond sorbet

Servings: 1 servings

Ingredient

- 1 cup Blanched almonds; toasted
- 2 cups Spring water
- ¾ cup Sugar
- 1 pinch Cinnamon
- 6 tablespoons Light corn syrup
- 2 tablespoons Amaretto
- 1 teaspoon Lemon zest

Directions:

a) In a food processor, grind the almonds to a powder. In a large saucepan, combine the water, sugar, corn syrup, liquor, zest, and cinnamon, then add the ground nuts.

b) Over medium heat, stir constantly until the sugar dissolves and the mixture boils. 2 minutes at a boil

c) Set aside to cool Using an ice cream maker, churn the mixture until it is semi-frozen.

d) If you don't have an ice cream maker, transfer the mixture to a stainless steel bowl and freeze until hard, stirring every 2 hours.

11.   Spanish apple torte

Servings: 8 Servings

Ingredient

- ¼ pounds Butter
- ½ cup Sugar
- 1 Egg yolk
- 1½ cup Sifted flour
- 1 dash Salt
- ⅛ teaspoon Baking powder
- 1 cup Milk
- ½ Lemon peel
- 3 Egg yolks
- ¼ cup Sugar
- ¼ cup Flour
- 1½ tablespoon Butter
- ¼ cup Sugar
- 1 tablespoon Lemon juice
- ½ teaspoon Cinnamon
- 4 Apples, peeled and sliced
- Apple; apricot, or any jelly of choice

Directions:

a) Preheat the oven to 350°F. Combine the sugar and butter in a mixing bowl. Mix together the remaining **Ingredients** until a ball forms.

b) Roll out the dough into a spring-form pan or a pie tin. Keep refrigerated until ready to use.

c) Combine the lemon juice, cinnamon, and sugar in a mixing bowl. Toss in with the apples and toss to coat. This is something that can be done ahead of time.

d) Add the lemon peel to the milk. Bring the milk to a boil, then reduce to a low heat for 10 minutes. Meanwhile, in a heavy sauce pan, whisk together the egg yolks and sugar.

e) When the milk is ready, slowly pour it into the yolk mixture while constantly whisking over low heat. Slowly mix in the flour while whisking over a low heat.

f) Continue to whisk the mixture until it is smooth and thick. Remove the pan from the heat. Slowly stir in the butter until it has melted.

g) Fill the crust with the custard. To make a single or double layer, place the apples on top. Place the torte in a 350°F oven for about 1 hour after it is finished.

h) Remove and set aside to cool. When the apples are cool enough to handle, warm the jelly of your choice and drizzle it over the top.

i) Set the jelly aside to cool. Serve.

12. Caramel custard

Servings: 1 Servings

Ingredient

- ½ cup Granulated sugar
- 1 teaspoon Water
- 4 Egg yolks or 3 whole eggs
- 2 cups Milk, scalded
- ½ teaspoon Vanilla extract

Directions:

a) In a large skillet, combine 6 tablespoons sugar and 1 cup water. Heat over low heat, shaking or swirling occasionally with a wooden spoon, until the sugar turns golden.

b) Pour the caramel syrup into a baking dish as soon as possible. Allow to cool until hard.

c) Preheat the oven to 325 degrees Fahrenheit.

d) Either beat the egg yolks or the whole eggs together. Mix in the milk, vanilla extract, and the remaining sugar until completely combined. Pour the cooled caramel on top.

e) Place the baking dish in a hot water bath. Bake for 1-112 hours, or until the center is set. Cool, cool, cool.

f) To serve, invert onto a serving plate with care.

13.   Spanish cheesecake

Servings: 10 servings

Ingredient

- 1 pounds Cream Cheese
- 1½ cup Sugar; Granulated
- 2 eggs
- ½ teaspoon Cinnamon; Ground
- 1 teaspoon Lemon Rind; Grated
- ¼ cup Unbleached Flour
- ½ teaspoon Salt
- 1 x Confectioners' Sugar
- 3 tablespoons Butter

Directions:

a) Preheat oven to 400 degrees Fahrenheit. Cream together the cheese, 1 tablespoon butter, and the sugar in a large mixing basin. Do not thrash.

b) Add the eggs one at a time, beating thoroughly after each addition.

c) Combine the cinnamon, lemon rind, flour, and salt. Butter the pan with the remaining 2 tablespoons of butter, spreading it evenly with your fingers.

d) Pour the batter into the prepared pan and bake at 400 degrees for 12 minutes, then decrease to 350 degrees and bake for another 25 to 30 minutes. The knife should be free of any residue.

e) When the cake has cooled to room temperature, dust it with confectioners' sugar.

14. Spanish fried custard

Servings: 8 servings

Ingredient

- 1 Cinnamon stick
- Peel of 1 lemon
- 3 cups Milk
- 1 cup Sugar
- 2 tablespoons Cornstarch
- 2 teaspoons Cinnamon
- Flour; for dredging
- Egg wash
- Olive oil; for frying

Directions:

a) Combine the cinnamon stick, lemon peel, 34 cup sugar, and 212 cups milk in a pot over medium heat.

b) Bring to a low boil, then reduce to a low heat and cook for 30 minutes. Remove the lemon peel and cinnamon stick. Combine the remaining milk and cornstarch in a small mixing basin.

c) Whisk thoroughly. In a slow, steady stream, stir the cornstarch mixture into the heated milk. Bring to a boil, then reduce to a low heat and cook for 8 minutes, whisking frequently. Remove from the fire and pour into an 8-inch baking dish that has been buttered.

d) Allow to cool completely. Cover and chill until completely cooled. Make 2-inch triangles out of the custard.

e) Combine the remaining 14 cup sugar and the cinnamon in a mixing bowl. Mix thoroughly. Dredge the triangles in flour until totally covered.

f) Dip each triangle in the egg wash and drip off any excess. Return the custards to the flour and coat completely.

g) Heat the oil in a large sauté pan over medium heat. Place the triangles in the hot oil and fry for 3 minutes, or until brown on both sides.

h) Remove the chicken from the pan and drain on paper towels. Toss with the cinnamon sugar mixture and season with salt and pepper.

i) Carry on with the rest of the triangles in the same manner.

15. Italian baked peaches

Servings: 1 Servings

Ingredient

- 6 Ripe peaches
- ⅓ cup Sugar
- 1 cup Ground almonds
- 1 Egg yolk
- ½ teaspoon Almond extract
- 4 tablespoons Butter
- ¼ cup Sliced almonds
- Heavy cream, optional

Directions:

a) Preheat the oven to 350 degrees Fahrenheit. Peaches should be rinsed, halved, and pitted. In a food processor, puree 2 of the peach halves.

b) In a mixing dish, combine the puree, sugar, ground almonds, egg yolk, and almond extract. To make a smooth paste, combine all of the ingredients in a mixing bowl.

c) Pour the filling over each peach half and set the filled peach halves in a buttered baking tray.

d) Sprinkle with sliced almonds and brush the remaining butter over the peaches before baking for 45 minutes.

e) Serve hot or cold, with a side of cream or ice cream.

16.   Spicy Italian prune-plum cake

Servings: 12 servings

Ingredient

- 2 cups Pitted and quartered Italian
- Prune-plums, cooked until
- Soft and cooled
- 1 cup Unsalted butter, softened
- 1¾ cup Granulated sugar
- 4 Eggs
- 3 cups Sifted flour
- ¼ cup Unsalted butter
- ½ pounds Powdered sugar
- 1½ tablespoon Unsweetened cocoa
- Pinch salt
- 1 teaspoon Cinnamon
- ½ teaspoon Ground cloves
- ½ teaspoon Ground nutmeg
- 2 teaspoons Baking soda
- ½ cup Milk
- 1 cup Walnuts, finely chopped
- 2 To 3 tablespoons strong, hot

- Coffee
- ¾ teaspoon Vanilla

Directions:

a) Preheat oven to 350°F. Butter and flour a 10-inch Bundt pan.

b) In a large mixing basin, cream together the butter and sugar until light and fluffy.

c) Beat in the eggs one by one.

d) Combine flour, spices, and baking soda in a sifter. In thirds, add the flour mixture to the butter mixture, alternating with the milk. Only beat to combine the ingredients.

e) Add the cooked prune-plums and walnuts and stir to combine. Turn into prepared pan and bake for 1 hour in a 350°F oven, or until cake begins to shrink from pan sides.

f) To make the frosting, cream together the butter and confectioners' sugar. Gradually add the sugar and cocoa powder, stirring constantly until completely combined. Season with salt.

g) Stir in a small amount of coffee at a time.

h) Beat till light and fluffy, then add vanilla and decorate the cake.

17. Spanish nut candy

Servings: 1 Servings

Ingredient

- 1 cup Milk
- 3 cups Light brown sugar
- 1 Tablespoon butter
- 1 teaspoon Vanilla extract
- 1 pounds walnut meats; chopped

Directions:

a) Boil the milk with the brown sugar until it caramelizes, then add the butter and vanilla essence right before serving.

b) Just before removing the candy from the fire, add the walnuts.

c) In a large mixing bowl, thoroughly combine the nuts and spoon the mixture into prepared muffin tins.

d) Cut into squares with a sharp knife right away.

18.   Honeyed pudding

Servings: 6 servings

Ingredient

- ¼ cup Unsalted butter
- 1½ cup Milk
- 2 large Eggs; lightly beaten
- 6 slices White country bread; torn
- ½ cup Clear; thin honey, plus
- 1 tablespoon Clear; thin honey
- ½ cup Hot water; plus
- 1 tablespoon Hot water
- ¼ teaspoon Ground cinnamon
- ¼ teaspoon Vanilla

Directions:

a) Preheat the oven to 350 degrees and use a little of the butter to butter a 9-inch glass pie dish. Whisk together the milk and eggs, then add the bread pieces and turn to coat them evenly.

b) Leave the bread to soak for 15 to 20 minutes, turning over once or twice. In a large non-stick skillet, heat the remaining butter over medium heat.

c) Fry the soaked bread in the butter until golden, about 2 to 3 minutes on each side. Transfer the bread to the baking dish.

d) In a bowl, combine the honey and the hot water and stir until the mixture is evenly blended.

e) Stir in the cinnamon and vanilla and drizzle the mixture over and around the bread.

f) Bake for about 30 minutes, or until golden brown.

19.   Spanish onion torte

Servings: 2 servings

Ingredient

- ½ teaspoon Olive oil
- 1 litre Spanish onions
- ¼ cup Water
- ¼ cup Red wine
- ¼ teaspoon Dried rosemary
- 250 grams Potatoes
- 3/16 cup Natural yoghurt
- ½ tablespoon Plain flour
- ½ Egg
- ¼ cup Parmesan cheese
- ⅛ cup Chopped Italian parsley

Directions:

a) Prepare the Spanish onions by thinly slicing them and grating the potatoes and parmesan cheese.

b) In a heavy-bottomed pan, heat the oil. Cook, stirring occasionally, until the onions are soft.

c) Simmer for 20 minutes, or until the liquid has evaporated and the onions have turned a dark-reddish brown color.

d) Mix the rosemary, potatoes, flour, yoghurt, egg, and parmesan cheese together in a mixing bowl. Toss in the onions.

e) In a well-greased 25cm ovenproof flan dish, spread the ingredients evenly. Preheat oven to 200°C and bake for 35-40 minutes, or until golden brown.

f) Garnish with parsley before cutting into wedges and serving.

20. Spanish pan soufflé

Servings: 1

Ingredient

- 1 Box Spanish Quick Brown Rice
- 4 Eggs
- 4 ounces Chopped green chilies
- 1 cup Water
- 1 cup Grated cheese

Directions:

a) Follow the packaging Directions for cooking the contents of the box.

b) When the rice is done, whisk in the remaining Ingredients, excluding the cheese.

c) Top with grated cheese and bake at 325°F for 30-35 minutes.

21.   Frozen Honey Semifreddo

Serves: 8 servings

Ingredients

- 8 ounces' heavy cream
- 1 teaspoon vanilla extract
- 1/4 teaspoon rose water
- 4 large eggs
- 4 1/2 ounces' honey
- 1/4 teaspoon plus 1/8 teaspoon kosher salt
- Toppings such as sliced fruit, toasted nuts, cocoa nibs, or shaved chocolate

Directions

a) Preheat oven to 350°F. Line a 9-by-5-inch loaf pan with plastic wrap or parchment paper.

b) For the Semifreddo, in the bowl of a stand mixer fitted with a whisk attachment, beat the cream, vanilla, and rose water until stiff.

c) Transfer to a separate bowl or plate, cover, and chill until ready to use.

d) In the bowl of a stand mixer, whisk together the eggs, honey, and salt. To blend, use a flexible spatula to stir everything together. Adjust heat to maintain a slow simmer over the prepared water bath, making sure the bowl does not touch the water.

e) In a stainless steel basin, cook, swirling and scraping regularly with a flexible spatula, until warmed to 165°F, about 10 minutes.

f) Transfer the mixture to a stand mixer fitted with a whisk attachment once it reaches 165°F. Whip the eggs on high until they are frothy.

g) Gently whisk in half of the prepared whipped cream by hand. Add the remaining Ingredients, whisk quickly, then fold in with a flexible spatula until well blended.

h) Scrape into prepared loaf pan, cover tightly, and freeze for 8 hours or until solid enough to slice, or until internal temperature reaches 0°F.

i) Invert the semifreddo onto a cooled dish to serve.

22.   Cilantro infused avocado lime sorbet

Makes 4
Total Time: 18 minutes

Ingredients

- 2 Avocados (Pit and Skin Removed)
- 1/4 cup Erythritol, Powdered
- 2 medium Limes, Juiced and Zested
- 1 cup Coconut Milk
- 1/4 teaspoons Liquid Stevia
- 1/4 - 1/2 cup Cilantro, Chopped

Directions

a) Bring Coconut Milk to a boil in a saucepan. Add the lime zest.

b) Allow the mixture to cool and then freeze.

c) In a food processor, combine the avocado, cilantro, and lime juice. Pulse until the mixture has a chunky texture.

d) Pour the coconut milk mixture and liquid stevia over the avocados. Pulse the mixture together until it reaches the appropriate consistency. It takes roughly 2-3 minutes to do this task.

e) Return to freezer to thaw or serve right away!

23. Pumpkin pie cheesecake

Makes 1

Total Time: 20 minutes

Ingredients

The Crust
- 3/4 cup Almond Flour
- 1/2 cup Flaxseed Meal
- 1/4 cup Butter
- 1 teaspoons Pumpkin Pie Spice
- 25 drops Liquid Stevia

The Filling
g) 6 oz. Vegan Cream Cheese
h) 1/3 cup Pumpkin Puree
i) 2 Tablespoons Sour Cream
j) 1/4 cup Vegan Heavy Cream
k) 3 Tablespoons Butter
l) 1/4 teaspoons Pumpkin Pie Spice
m) 25 drops Liquid Stevia

Directions

a) Combine all the crust's dry ingredients and stir thoroughly.

b) Mash together the dry ingredients with the butter and liquid stevia until a dough forms.

c) For your mini tart pans, roll the dough into little spheres.

d) Press the dough against the side of the tart pan until it reaches and goes up the sides.

e) Combine all the filling ingredients in a mixing bowl.

f) Blend the filling ingredients together using an immersion blender.

g) Once the filling ingredients are smooth, distribute them into the crust and chill.

h) Remove from the fridge, slice, and top with whipped cream if desired.

24.   Mocha ice cream

Makes 2
Total Time: 10 minutes

Ingredients

- 1 cup Coconut Milk
- 1/4 cup Vegan Heavy Cream
- 2 Tablespoons Erythritol
- 20 drops Liquid Stevia
- 2 Tablespoons Cocoa Powder
- 1 Tablespoons Instant Coffee
- Mint

Directions

a) Blend all ingredients and then transfer to your ice cream maker and churn according to the manufacturer's instructions for 15-20 minutes.

b) When ice cream is softly frozen, serve immediately with a mint leaf.

25.   Cherry and chocolate donuts

Makes 12

Ingredients

Dry Ingredients

- 3/4 cup Almond Flour
- 1/4 cup Golden Flaxseed Meal
- 1 teaspoons Baking Powder
- Pinch Salt
- 10g bars Dark Chocolate, diced into chunks

Wet Ingredients

- 2 large Eggs
- 1 teaspoons Vanilla Extract
- 2 1/2 Tablespoons Coconut Oil
- 3 Tablespoons Coconut Milk

Directions

a) In a large mixing bowl, combine the dry ingredients (except the dark chocolate).

b) Mix in the wet ingredients and then fold in the dark Chocolate chunks.

c) Plug in your doughnut maker and oil it if necessary.

d) Pour the batter into the donut maker, close and cook about 4-5 minutes.

e) Reduce the heat to low and cook for another 2-3 minutes.

f) Repeat for the rest of the batter and then serve.

26. Blackberry pudding

Makes 1

Ingredients

- 1/4 cup Coconut Flour
- 1/4 teaspoons Baking Powder
- 2 Tablespoons Coconut Oil
- 2 Tablespoons Vegan Butter
- 2 Tablespoons Vegan Heavy Cream
- 2 teaspoons Lemon Juice
- Zest 1 Lemon
- 1/4 cup Blackberries
- 2 Tablespoons Erythritol
- 20 drops Liquid Stevia

Directions

a) Preheat the oven to 350 degrees Fahrenheit.

b) Sift the dry ingredients over the wet components and mix on low speed until thoroughly combined.

c) Divide the batter between two ramekins.

d) Push the blackberries into the top of the batter to equally distribute them in the batter.

e) Bake for 20-25 minutes.

f) Serve with a dollop of heavy whipping cream on top!

27.   Pumpkin Pie with Maple syrup

Makes 8 servings

Ingredients

- 1 vegan pie crust
- 1 (16-ounce) can solid pack pumpkin
- 1 (12-ounce) package extra-firm silken tofu, drained and patted dry
- 1 cup sugar
- 2 teaspoons ground cinnamon
- 1/2 teaspoon ground allspice
- 1/2 teaspoon ground ginger
- 1/2 teaspoon ground nutmeg

Directions

a) Blend the pumpkin and tofu in a food processor until smooth. Add the sugar, maple syrup, cinnamon, allspice, ginger, and nutmeg until smooth.

b) Preheat the oven to 400 degrees Fahrenheit.

c) Fill the crust with the filling. Bake for 15 minutes at 350°F.

28.Rustic Cottage Pie

Makes 4 to 6 servings

Ingredients

- Yukon Gold potatoes, peeled and diced
- 2 tablespoons vegan margarine
- 1/4 cup plain unsweetened soy milk
- Salt and freshly ground black pepper
- 1 tablespoon olive oil
- 1 medium yellow onion, finely chopped
- 1 medium carrot, finely chopped
- 1 celery rib, finely chopped
- 12 ounces seitan, finely chopped
- 1 cup frozen peas
- 1 cup frozen corn kernels
- 1 teaspoon dried savory
- 1/2 teaspoon dried thyme

Directions

a) In a saucepan of boiling salted water, cook the potatoes until tender, 15 to 20 minutes.

b) Drain well and return to the pot. Add the margarine, soy milk, and salt and pepper to taste.

c) Coarsely mash with a potato masher and set aside. Preheat the oven to 350°F.

d) In a large skillet, heat the oil over medium heat. Add the onion, carrot, and celery.

e) Cover and cook until tender, about 10 minutes. Transfer the vegetables to a 9 x 13-inch baking pan. Stir in the seitan, mushroom sauce, peas, corn, savory, and thyme.

f) Season with salt and pepper to taste and spread the mixture evenly in the baking pan.

g) Top with the mashed potatoes, spreading to the edges of the baking pan. Bake until the potatoes are browned and the filling is bubbly, about 45 minutes.

h) Serve immediately.

29.   Chocolate amaretto fondue

Makes 4 Servings

Ingredients

- 3 ounces unsweetened baking chocolate
- 1 cup heavy cream
- 24 packets aspartame sweetener
- 1 tablespoon sugar
- 1 teaspoon amaretto
- 1 teaspoon vanilla extract
- Berries, ½ cup per serving

Directions

a) Break the chocolate into small pieces and place in a 2-cup glass measure with the cream.

b) Heat in the microwave on high until the chocolate is melted, about 2 minutes. Whisk until the mixture is shiny.

c) Add the sweetener, sugar, amaretto, and vanilla, whisking until the mixture is smooth.

d) Transfer the mixture to a fondue pot or a serving bowl. Serve with berries for dipping.

30. Flans with a raspberry coulis

Makes 2 to 4 servings

Ingredients

- 1 cup milk
- 1 cup half-and-half
- 2 large eggs
- 2 large egg yolks
- 6 packets aspartame sweetener
- $\frac{1}{4}$ teaspoon kosher salt
- 1 teaspoon vanilla extract
- 1 cup fresh raspberries

Directions

a) Place a roasting pan filled with 1 inch of water on a rack in the lower third of the oven.

b) Butter six $\frac{1}{2}$-inch ramekins. Heat the milk and half-and-half in the microwave on high (100 percent power) for 2 minutes or on the stovetop in a medium saucepan until warm.

c) Meanwhile, beat the eggs and egg yolks in a medium bowl until foamy.

d) Gradually whisk the hot milk mixture into the eggs. Stir in the sweetener, salt, and vanilla. Pour the mixture into the prepared ramekins.

e) Place in the water-filled saucepans and bake until the custards are set, about 30 minutes.

f) Remove the dishes from the roasting pan and cool to room temperature on a wire rack, then refrigerate until chilled, about 2 hours.

g) To make the coulis, simply purée the raspberries in the food processor. Add sweetener to taste.

h) To serve, run a spoon around the edge of each custard and turn it out onto a dessert plate.

i) Drizzle coulis over the top of the custard and finish with a few fresh raspberries and a sprig of mint, if using.

31.   Fruit balls in bourbon

Makes 2 servings

Ingredients

- ½ cup melon balls
- ½ cup halved strawberries
- 1 tablespoon bourbon
- 1 tablespoon sugar
- ½ packet aspartame sweetener
- Sprigs of fresh mint for garnish

Directions

a) Combine the melon balls and strawberries in a glass dish.

b) Toss with the bourbon, sugar, and aspartame.

c) Cover and refrigerate until serving time. Spoon the fruit into dessert dishes and decorate with mint leaves.

32.   Pecan Pie Ice Cream

Yield: 5 Cups

Ingredients:

- 2 cups whole milk
- 1 cup heavy cream
- ½ cup light brown sugar
- 2 eggs
- 1 teaspoon vanilla extract
- 1 cup coarsely chopped pecans
- ⅔ cup maple syrup
- 2 tablespoons melted unsalted butter
- ¼ teaspoon kosher salt

Directions:

a) In a large pot, combine the milk and cream. Add the sugar and mix well. Heat over medium-high heat until scalded.

b) In a small mixing bowl, whisk together the eggs until well combined. Whisk a few tablespoons of the hot milk mixture into the eggs, then slowly pour the egg mixture back into the pan.

c) As the mixture cools, continue stirring for another 5 minutes or more. Mix in the vanilla extract.

d) Spoon the custard into a bowl, cover, and chill for 6 hours or overnight.

e) In a small, heavy skillet, toast the pecans over medium-high heat. Stir them around until they're gently browned. Remove the pan from the heat. Add the maple syrup, butter, and salt to taste.

f) Stir to evenly coat pecans. Refrigerate the mixture.

g) Pour the chilled custard into your ice cream machine and churn for 40 to 50 minutes, or until the mixture has the consistency of soft ice cream.

h) Place it in a mixing dish. Swirl in the cooled nuts and syrup.

i) Freeze the ice cream in one or more containers for at least 2 hours, or until firm.

33. Cinnamon Chip Bread Pudding

Yield: 10 Servings

Ingredients

Bread Pudding:

- 2 cups Half-and-half
- 2 Tablespoons butter
- 3 eggs
- 1/3 cup sugar
- 1/4 teaspoons ground nutmeg
- 1 teaspoons vanilla extract
- 3 cups of bread, torn into small pieces
- A handful of cinnamon chips

Vanilla Milk:

- 1 cup milk
- 1/4 cup butter
- 1/3 cup sugar
- 1 teaspoons vanilla
- 1Tablespoons flour

- 1/2 teaspoons salt

Directions:
Bread Pudding:

a) Simmer Half and Half and butter in a saucepan over medium-high heat.

b) In a separate dish, whisk together the eggs, nutmeg, and vanilla extract. Beat in the heated milk and butter mixture thoroughly.

c) Tear bread into small pieces and place in a casserole dish that has been prepared.

d) Spread the mixture on top and top with cinnamon chips.

e) Cover with foil and bake for 30 minutes at 350 degrees.

f) Remove the foil and bake for another 15 minutes.

Warm Vanilla Milk:

g) Melt the butter and mix in the flour to make a paste.

h) Add the milk, sugar, vanilla, and salt and bring to a boil, stirring frequently, for 5 minutes, or until it thickens into a syrup.

i) Pour the sauce over the warm bread pudding and serve immediately.

34.   Baked Caramel Apples

Yield: 24 Apples

Ingredients:

- 24 apples peeled, cored, cut into chunks
- 3 cups brown sugar
- 3/4 cup water
- 6 Tablespoons butter
- 3 teaspoons salt
- 6 Tablespoons flour
- extra butter for dotting
- sprinkle of cinnamon

Directions:

a) Preheat the oven to 350 degrees Fahrenheit.

b) In a saucepan, combine all sauce ingredients and bring to a soft boil; the sauce will thicken and convert into a caramel/gravy texture.

c) Distribute apples evenly between two 9x13-inch baking plates, then cover with equal amounts of caramel sauce.

d) Spread butter over top and sprinkle cinnamon on top.

e) Bake covered for 1 hour, stirring after 30 minutes.

35.   Give Thanks Pumpkin Pie

Yield: 8 Servings

Ingredients:

- 1 can (30 oz.) Pumpkin Pie Mix
- 2/3 cup Evaporated Milk
- 2 large eggs, beaten
- 1 unbaked 9-inch pie shell

Directions:

a) Preheat the oven to 425 degrees Fahrenheit.

b) In a large mixing bowl, combine the pumpkin pie mix, evaporated milk, and eggs.

c) Pour the filling into the pie shell.

d) Bake for 15 minutes in the oven.

e) Raise the temperature to 350°F and bake for another 50 minutes.

f) Give it a gentle shake to see if it's fully baked.

g) Cool for 2 hours on a wire rack.

36. Low Fat Pumpkin Trifle

Yield: 18 Servings

Ingredients:

Cake:

- 1 box Spice Cake, crumbled with hands
- 1 1/4 cups water
- 1 egg

Pudding Filling:

- 4 cups skim milk
- 4 packages (1 oz. each) butterscotch pudding mix
- 1 can (15 oz.) pumpkin mix
- 1 1/2 teaspoons Pumpkin Spice
- 12 ounces light whipped topping

Directions:

a) Combine all the cake ingredients in an 8-inch square baking pan and bake for 35 minutes, or until set.

b) Cool on stove or wire rack.

c) In a large mixing bowl, combine milk and pudding mix. Allow to thicken for a few minutes. Mix in the pumpkin and spices thoroughly.

d) Start by layering a fourth of the cake, then half of the pumpkin mixture, then a fourth of the cake and half the whipped cream

e) Repeat the layers

f) Garnish with whipped topping and cake crumbs. Refrigerate until ready to serve

37. Pumpkin Dump Cake

Yield: 10 Servings

Ingredients:

- 1 -30 oz. pumpkin pie puree
- 2 eggs
- 1 can evaporated milk
- 1/2 box yellow cake mix
- 1 cup chopped walnuts
- 1/2 cup butter

Directions:

a) Preheat the oven to 350 degrees Fahrenheit.

b) Using a mixer, thoroughly combine pumpkin pie puree, eggs, and milk.

c) Pour the ingredients into an 11x7 or 8x8 pan.

d) Slightly whisk in 1/2 box of dry cake mix on top.

e) Top with chopped walnuts and 1/2 cup melted butter.

f) Bake for about 40 minutes.

g) Leave to cool until ready to serve.

h) Add whipped cream on top.

38. Chia Pudding

Yield: 4 desert bowls

Ingredients
- 1 can organic coconut milk and 1 can of water, combined
- 8 tablespoons of chia seed
- 1/2 teaspoonful organic vanilla extract
- 2 tablespoons brown rice syrup

Directions:

a) Mix together coconut milk, water, brown rice syrup, and chia seed in a mixing bowl.

b) Mix everything together for ten minutes.

c) Refrigerate for 30 minutes before serving.

d) Insert 1 teaspoon of ground vanilla or 1/2 teaspoon of organic vanilla extract into the mixture.

e) Spoon into dessert bowls and sprinkle with vanilla powder or freshly ground nutmeg.

f) Letting it sit overnight gives it a solid texture.

39. Apple Treats

Yield: 6 Biscuits

Ingredients
- 1 cup almond, soak overnight
- 1 ½ cup crunchy apples
- ½ cup flax seeds – ground
- 2 large dates, pitted and de-stemmed
- 1 tablespoon lemon juice
- 1 teaspoon Grey sea salt
- ½ cup psyllium husk

Directions:

a) Blend the almonds, salt, lemon juice, dates, and apples in a food processor. Add the flax seed and psyllium husk.

b) Scoop out golf ball-sized parts of the dough, roll them into balls, and arrange them on a dehydrator sheet with 1 inch between them.

c) Pat the rounded tops down.

d) Dehydrate overnight in the dehydrator, or bake for 1 hour at the lowest setting with the door slightly ajar.

e) Remove the fruit and protein snacks and check for firmness.

40. Butternut Squash Mousse

Yield: 4 Servings

Ingredients
- 2 cups butternut squash, peeled and cubed
- 1 cup water
- 1 teaspoon lemon juice
- 1 cup cashews or pine nuts
- 4 dates – pitted and stems removed
- ½ teaspoon cinnamon
- 1 teaspoon nutmeg
- 2 teaspoons organic vanilla extract

Directions:
a) In a blender, combine all ingredients and blend for roughly 5 minutes, or until well combined.

b) Transfer to individual serving cups or a big serving dish.

c) This can be left in the refrigerator overnight, and the flavors will blend together, making it even more spicy.

d) Drizzle with maple syrup before serving.

41. Southern Sweet Potato Pie

Yield: 10 Servings

Ingredients:

- 2 cups peeled, cooked sweet potatoes
- ¼ cup melted butter
- 2 eggs
- 1 cup sugar
- 2 tablespoons bourbon
- 1/4 teaspoon salt
- 1/4 teaspoon ground cinnamon
- 1/4 teaspoon ground ginger
- 1 cup milk

Directions:

a) Preheat oven to 350 degrees Fahrenheit.

b) With the exception of the milk, fully combine all of the ingredients in an electric mixer.

c) Add the milk and continue to stir once everything is fully combined.

d) Pour the filling into the pie shell and bake for 35-45 minutes, or until a knife inserted near the center comes out clean.

e) Remove from the refrigerator and allow it cool to room temperature before serving.

42.   Sweet Potato and Coffee Brownies

Yield: 8

Ingredients:

- 1/3 cup freshly brewed hot coffee
- 1-ounce unsweetened chocolate, chopped
- 1/4 cup canola oil
- 2/3 cup sweet potato purée
- 2 teaspoons pure vanilla extract

Directions:

a) Preheat the oven to 350 degrees Fahrenheit.

b) In a small bowl, combine the coffee and 1-ounce chocolate and let aside for 1 minute.

c) In a large mixing bowl, combine the oil, sweet potato purée, vanilla extract, sugar, cocoa powder, and salt. Mix until everything is well blended.

d) Combine the flour and baking powder in a separate bowl. Add the chocolate chips and mix well.

e) Using a spatula, gently stir the dry ingredients into the wet ones until all of the ingredients are combined.

f) Pour the batter into the baking dish and bake for 30-35 minutes, or until a toothpick inserted in the center comes out clean.

g) Allow to cool completely.

43. Thanksgiving Corn Soufflé

Yield: 8-10 Servings

Ingredients:

- 1 medium onion
- 5 lbs. frozen sweet corn
- 6 cups Monterey Jack, shredded
- 3 eggs
- 1 teaspoons salt

Directions:

a) In a skillet, sauté the onion in olive oil. Set aside.

b) In a food processor, grind corn.

c) Combine and stir in the other ingredients, including the sautéed onion.

d) Place in an 8x14 baking dish that has been buttered.

e) Bake at 375°F for about 25 minutes, or until the top is golden brown.

44. Cranberry Ice Cream

Yield: 2 Servings

Ingredients:

Cranberry Puree

- 1/4 Cup Water
- 1/4 teaspoons Salt
- 12 oz. Fresh Cranberries, cleaned and sorted
- 2 Tb Fresh Squeezed Orange Juice

Ice Cream

- 1½ Cups Heavy Cream
- 1½ Cups Whole Milk
- 1 Cup Sugar
- 1¼ Cups Cranberry Puree

Directions:

Cranberry Puree:

a) Heat the water, salt, and cranberries for 6-7 minutes over medium heat.

b) Remove from heat and set aside for 10 minutes to cool.

c) In a blender or food processor, puree the cranberries and orange juice.

d) Refrigerate the cranberry puree for several hours.

Ice Cream

e) Combine the cream, milk, sugar, and cranberry puree in a mixing bowl.

f) In an ice cream machine, churn the ingredients according to the manufacturer's directions.

g) Transfer the frozen and creamy mixture to a chilled ice cream container.

h) Freeze for a minimum of 4-6 hours.

i) Thaw in the refrigerator for 5-10 minutes before serving.

45.   Walnut Petites

Yield: 4 Dozen

Ingredients:

- 8 oz. cream cheese, softened
- 1cup unsalted butter, softened
- 2 cups all-purpose flour
- 2 large eggs
- 1 1/2 cup packed brown sugar
- 2 cups chopped walnuts

Directions:

a) Preheat the oven to 350 degrees Fahrenheit.

b) Using an electric mixer, beat cream cheese and butter until smooth.

c) Sift in the flour and a bit of salt, then stir until the dough forms. Cut into four doughs and refrigerate for at least 1 hour, wrapped in plastic wraps.

d) Roll each piece of dough into 12 balls and press each ball into the bottom and up the edges of a mini-muffin cup to produce a pastry shell. Refrigerate until ready to use.

e) In a large mixing bowl, whisk together the eggs, brown sugar, and a pinch of salt until smooth, then fold in the walnuts.

f) Put 1 spoonful of filling in each pastry shell

g) Bake in batches in the middle of the oven for 25 to 30 minutes, or until the filling is bubbling and the pastry is light golden.

h) Transfer to a cooling rack.

46.   Thanksgiving Carrot Soufflé

Yield: 8 Servings

Ingredients:

- 2lbs. fresh carrots, peeled and boiled
- 6 eggs
- 2/3 cup sugar
- 6 Tablespoons matzoh meal
- 2 teaspoons vanilla
- 2 sticks butter or margarine, melted
- Dash of nutmeg
- 6 Tablespoons brown sugar
- 4 Tablespoons butter or margarine, melted
- 1 cup chopped walnuts

Directions:

a) Puree the carrots and eggs in a food processor.

b) Process the next five ingredients until smooth.

c) Bake for 40 minutes in a greased 9x13 baking pan at 350°F.

d) Add the topping and bake for another 5-10 minutes.

47. Pumpkin Flan

Yield: 6-8 Servings

Ingredients:

- ¾ cup sugar
- ½ teaspoons pure maple extract
- 2 teaspoons grated orange zest (2 oranges)
- ½ teaspoon fleur de sel
- 1½ teaspoons ground cinnamon
- 1 (14 oz.) can sweetened condensed milk
- ½ teaspoons ground nutmeg
- 1 (12 oz.) can evaporated milk
- 1 cup pumpkin puree
- ½ cup (4 oz.) Italian mascarpone
- 4 extra-large eggs
- 1 teaspoon pure vanilla extract

Directions:

a) Make the caramel: In a small, heavy-bottomed saucepan, combine the sugar, maple syrup, and 1/3 cup water.

b) Cook at a low boil, stirring occasionally, for 5-10 minutes, or until the mixture turns golden brown and reaches 230°F.

c) Take the pan off the heat, whisk in the fleur de sel, and pour into a big round cake pan right away.

d) In a mixing bowl, combine the condensed milk, evaporated milk, pumpkin puree, and mascarpone; beat on low speed until smooth.

e) Beat the eggs, vanilla, maple extract, orange zest, cinnamon, and nutmeg together in a mixing bowl. Pour the pumpkin mixture into the pan with the caramel slowly so that they do not mix.

f) Place the cake pan in a roasting pan and pour enough hot water into the roasting pan to come halfway up the edges of the cake pan.

g) Bake for 70-75 minutes in the center of the oven, until the custard is barely set.

h) Remove the flan from the water bath and cool fully on a cooling rack. Refrigerate for at least 3 hours.

i) Run a little knife around the flan's edge.

j) Flip the cake pan over onto a flat serving plate with a slight lip, and turn the flan out onto the plate. The caramel should drip over the sides of the flan.

k) Cut into wedges and serve with a spoonful of caramel on top of each slice.

48.   Country Corn Casserole

Yield: 4 Servings

Ingredients
- 2 cups corn kernels
- 1 teaspoon sugar
- 1 teaspoon vanilla extract
- 1 teaspoon salt
- 1/4 teaspoon black pepper
- 2 eggs, beaten
- 1 cup milk
- 1 tablespoon butter, melted
- 2 tablespoons cracker crumbs

Directions:
a) Preheat the oven to 350°F.

b) In a large mixing bowl, combine all ingredients.

c) Pour into an ungreased 1-1/2-quart casserole dish.

d) Bake for 40–50 minutes, or until golden brown.

49.   Cranberry Pecan Relish

Yield: 3 Cups

Ingredients

- 1 seedless orange, cut into large chunks
- 1 apple, cored and cut into large chunks
- 2 cups fresh cranberries
- 1/2 cup sugar
- 1/4 cup pecans

Directions

a) In a food processor, combine all of the ingredients.

b) Process for 1 to 2 minutes, scraping down the sides of the container as needed, or until finely chopped and completely blended.

c) Serve immediately, or chill until ready to serve in an airtight container.

50. Turkey and Potato Hash Cakes

Yield: 12 Cakes

Ingredients
- 2 cups mashed potatoes
- 4 cups finely chopped cooked turkey
- 1/4 cup chopped onions
- 1/4 cup chopped green bell peppers
- 1/4 cup dry bread crumbs
- 1 teaspoon salt
- 3/4 teaspoon black pepper
- 1/4 teaspoon garlic powder
- 1/4 teaspoon paprika
- 1/4 cup chopped parsley
- 3 eggs, slightly beaten
- 1/2 cup vegetable oil

Directions:
a) In a large mixing bowl, whisk together all of the ingredients except the oil.

b) Make pancakes out of the mixture.

c) Heat enough oil to coat a large skillet over medium-high heat; cook pancakes on each side, adding more oil as required, until golden brown, then drain on paper towels.

d) Serve immediately.

51. Apple Crunch Cobbler

Yield: 8 Servings

Ingredients
- 4 medium apples, peeled and sliced
- 2 cups granola cereal, divided
- 1/2 cup golden raisins
- 1/4 cup honey
- 1/4 cup packed brown sugar
- 2 tablespoons butter, melted
- 1 teaspoon vanilla extract
- 1 teaspoon ground cinnamon
- 1/4 teaspoon ground nutmeg
- 1/8 teaspoon ground cloves
- 8 cups vanilla ice cream

Directions:

a) In a 4-quart slow cooker, gently heat the apples.

b) In a medium mixing bowl, combine granola cereal and next 8 ingredients; sprinkle over apples.

c) Cook on LOW for 6 hours, covered.

d) Serve the apples on top of vanilla ice cream.

52.   Gooey Amish Caramel Pie

Yield: 8 Servings

Ingredients
- 2 cups light brown sugar
- 1 cup water
- 1 tablespoon butter
- 3/4 cup all-purpose flour
- 3/4 cup milk
- 3 egg yolks
- 1 teaspoon vanilla extract
- 1 (9-inch) baked pie crust
- 1 cup pecan halves

Directions:

a) Bring brown sugar, water, and butter to a boil in a medium saucepan over medium-high heat; simmer 3 to 5 minutes, stirring regularly.

b) In a medium mixing bowl, whisk together flour, milk, and egg yolks.

c) Slowly add flour mixture into boiling mixture for 3 to 5 minutes, stirring frequently.

d) Remove from the heat, mix in the vanilla extract, and set aside to cool for 5 minutes.

e) Pour the filling into a cooked pie crust and top with pecan halves.

f) Set aside for 30 minutes to cool before refrigerating for 8 hours or overnight.

53.   Autumn Leaves

Yield: 12 Leaves

Ingredients
- 1 rolled refrigerated pie crust
- 1 egg
- 2 tablespoons water

Directions:
a) Preheat the oven to 350°F.

b) Cut out leaf shapes from pie crust with a stencil, a sharp knife or cookie cutter.

c) Score lines on "leaf" cutouts with a knife to resemble veins on genuine leaves, but don't cut all the way through the crust.

d) To create a natural curve during baking, place cutouts on a cookie sheet or drape over bunched-up aluminum foil.

e) In a small mixing bowl, whisk together the egg and water until thoroughly blended. Brush the cutouts with egg wash.

f) Bake for 3 to 5 minutes, until golden.

54. Harvest Fruit Compote

Yield: 8 Servings

Ingredients

- 5 apples, cut into 1-inch chunks
- 3 medium pears, cut into 1-inch chunks
- 3 large oranges, peeled and sectioned
- 1 (12-ounce) package fresh cranberries
- 1 1/2 cups apple juice
- 1 1/2 cups packed light brown sugar

Directions:

a) Combine all ingredients in a soup pot and bring to a boil over medium-high heat.

b) Reduce heat to medium and cook, stirring periodically, for 10 to 15 minutes, or until fruit is soft.

c) After the fruit has cooled, spoon it into an airtight container and keep it there until ready to serve.

55. Thanksgiving cranberry pie

Yield: 8 Servings

Ingredients
- 2 pie crusts
- 1 pack gelatin; orange flavor
- ¾ cup Boiling water
- ½ cup Orange juice
- 1 can(8-oz) jellied cranberry sauce
- 1 teaspoon Grated orange rind
- 1 cup Cold Half-and-Half or milk
- 1 pack Jell-O instant pudding, French vanilla or vanilla flavor
- 1 cup Cool Whip whipped topping
- Frosted cranberries

Directions:
a) Preheat oven to 450°F

b) BRING gelatin to a boil and dissolve it. Pour in the orange juice. Place bowl in bigger ice and water bowl. Allow it sit for 5 minutes, stirring regularly, until gelatin has thickened slightly.

c) Add the cranberry sauce and orange rind and stir to combine. Fill the pie crust with the filling. Chill for about 30 minutes, or until set.

d) Into a medium mixing bowl, pour half and half. Toss in the pie filling mix. Whisk until completely mixed.

e) Set aside for 2 minutes, or until the sauce has thickened somewhat. Lastly, fold in the whipped topping.

f) Gently spread gelatin mixture on top. Chill for 2 hours or until stiff.

g) If preferred, top with more whipped topping and Frosted Cranberries.

56. Sparkling Cranberries

Yield: 2 Cups

Ingredients
- 1 cup pure maple syrup
- 2 cups fresh cranberries
- 1 cup sugar
- Parchment paper

Directions:

a) Cook maple syrup for 1 to 2 minutes in a saucepan over medium-low heat.

b) Take off the heat and mix in the cranberries.

c) Chill for 8 to 12 hours, covered.

d) Drain the cranberries.

e) Toss 4 to 5 cranberries into sugar at a time, gently tossing to coat.

f) Place cranberries in a single layer on a baking sheet coated with parchment paper and set aside to dry entirely.

57. Torte with lemon filling

Meringue shell
- 3 large egg whites
- ¼ teaspoon cream of tartar
- ¼ teaspoon kosher salt
- 10 packets aspartame sweetener

Filling
- 2¼ cups water
- Grated zest of 1 lemon plus juice
- 30 packets aspartame sweetener
- 1/3 cup plus 2 tablespoons cornstarch
- 2 large eggs and 2 large egg whites
- 2 tablespoons unsalted butter

Directions:

a) Beat the 3 egg whites in a medium bowl until foamy. Add the cream of tartar, salt, and sweetener and beat to stiff peaks. Line a baking sheet with parchment paper and pour the meringue onto the paper.

b) Mix the water, lemon zest and juice, salt, sweetener, and corn-starch in a medium saucepan. Bring to a boil over medium-high heat, stirring constantly.

c) Beat two eggs and two egg whites in a small bowl. Stir in about half of the hot cornstarch mixture, and then stir this egg mixture back into the cornstarch mixture remaining in the pan. Cook and stir over low heat for 1 minute.

d) Remove from The Heat and Swirl in The Butter. Pour The Mixture into The Cooked and Cooled Meringue Shell. Top with The Sliced Strawberries, And Serve at Once.

58. Chocolate amaretto fondue

Ingredients:
- 3 ounces unsweetened baking chocolate
- 1 cup heavy cream
- 24 packets aspartame sweetener
- 1 tablespoon sugar
- 1 teaspoon amaretto
- 1 teaspoon vanilla extract
- Berries of your choice, about $\frac{1}{2}$ cup per serving

Directions:

a) Break the chocolate into small pieces and place in a 2-cup glass measure with the cream. Heat in the microwave on high (100 percent power), until the chocolate is melted, about 2 minutes (or heat in a double-broiler over low heat, whisking constantly). Whisk until the mixture is shiny.

b) Add the sweetener, sugar, amaretto, and vanilla, whisking until the mixture is smooth.

c) Transfer the mixture to a fondue pot or a serving bowl. Serve with berries for dipping.

59.   Flans with a raspberry coulis

Ingredients:
- 1 cup milk
- 1 cup half-and-half
- 2 large eggs
- 2 large egg yolks
- 6 packets aspartame sweetener
- $\frac{1}{4}$ teaspoon kosher salt
- 1 teaspoon vanilla extract
- 1 cup fresh raspberries

Directions:

a) Place a roasting pan filled with 1 inch of water on a rack in the lower third of the oven.

b) Butter six $\frac{1}{2}$-inch ramekins. Heat the milk and half-and-half in the microwave on high (100 percent power) for 2 minutes or on the stovetop in a medium saucepan until warm.

c) Meanwhile, beat the eggs and egg yolks in a medium bowl until foamy. Gradually whisk the hot milk mixture into the eggs. Stir in the sweetener, salt, and vanilla. Pour the mixture into the prepared ramekins.

d) Place in the water-filled saucepans and bake until the custards are set, about 30 minutes.

e) Remove the dishes from the roasting pan and cool to room temperature on a wire rack, then refrigerate until chilled, about 2 hours.

f) To make the coulis, simply purée the raspberries in the food processor. Add sweetener to taste.

g) To serve, run a spoon around the edge of each custard and turn it out onto a dessert plate. Drizzle coulis over the top of the custard and finish with a few fresh raspberries and a sprig of mint, if using.

60. Chocolate cake

Ingredients:

- Cocoa for dusting the pan
- 6 tablespoons unsalted butter
- 4 ounces unsweetened chocolate
- 1/3 cup half-and-half
- 1/3 cup raspberry all-fruit preserves
- 1 teaspoon instant espresso powder
- 1 tablespoon sugar
- 3 large eggs, separated
- 1 teaspoon vanilla extract
- 22 packets aspartame sweetener
- $\frac{1}{8}$ teaspoon cream of tartar
- $\frac{1}{4}$ cup all-purpose flour
- $\frac{1}{8}$ teaspoon salt
- 1 cup heavy cream
- $\frac{1}{2}$ cup raspberries for garnish (optional)

Directions:

a) Combine the butter, chocolate, half-and-half, raspberry preserves, and espresso powder in a microwave-safe dish. Heat in the microwave on high (100 percent power) until the chocolate is melted, 2 to 3 minutes.

b) Whisk in the sugar, egg yolks, and vanilla. Add the aspartame, whisking until smooth.

c) In another bowl, beat the egg whites until foamy, then add the cream of tartar and beat to stiff peaks. Fold the chocolate mixture into the egg whites, and then fold in the combined flour and salt, taking care not to overmix. Pour into the prepared pan. Bake.

61. Flan almendra

Ingredients:

- 1¼ cups whole milk
- 4 large eggs
- 3 packets aspartame sweetener, or to taste
- 1 tablespoon sugar
- 1 teaspoon vanilla extract
- 1 teaspoon almond extract (optional)
- ¼ cup slivered almonds
- ½ cup berries of your choice for garnish (optional)

Directions:

a) Place a roasting pan filled with 1 inch of water in the oven and preheat to 325°F. Butter 4 ramekins or glass custard cups.

b) Warm the milk in a 1-quart, microwave-safe bowl for 2 minutes on high (100 percent power). Alternatively, heat on the stovetop in a medium saucepan to just under a boil.

c) Meanwhile, in another bowl, whisk together the eggs, sweetener, sugar, vanilla, and almond extract, if using. Pour the hot milk into the egg mixture and stir to blend.

d) Toast the almonds by heating them in a small dry skillet just until they begin to brown, about 1 minute. Divide the almonds among the 4 ramekins, then fill with the custard. Cover with aluminum foil. Place the ramekins in the water bath. Bake until the custards are set, about 20 minutes. To test, insert a knife in the middle; it should come out clean.

e) Serve at room temperature or chilled. To serve, run a knife around the edge of the ramekin, then turn out the flan onto a dessert plate. If you wish, add ½ cup of berries of your choice.

62. Spiced strawberries

Ingredients:
- 2 cups halved strawberries
- 1 tablespoon sugar
- 2 teaspoon sherry vinegar
- ¼ teaspoon finely milled black pepper

Directions:

a) Toss the berries with the sugar, vinegar, and pepper in a medium bowl. Cover and chill for at least 15 minutes.

b) Serve in footed dessert dishes.

63. Blackberry fool

Ingredients:

- 1 cup crème fraîche, or 1 tablespoon sour cream plus 1 cup heavy cream
- 1 cup blackberries
- 1 tablespoon sugar
- 1 packet aspartame sweetener, or to taste
- $\frac{1}{8}$ teaspoon crème de cassis

Directions:

a) Set aside 6 gorgeous blackberries. Combine the remaining berries with sugar, sweetener, crème de cassis, and crème fraîche. Gently mix, then spoon into footed dessert dishes.

b) Cover and chill until serving time. Garnish with the reserved berries.

64. Zabaglione

Ingredients:
- 6 large egg yolks
- 2 packets aspartame sweetener
- ¼ cup Marsala
- 1 tablespoon grated orange zest
- 3 tablespoons Grand Marnier
- 1 cup heavy cream, whipped to soft peaks

Directions:

a) Beat the egg yolks and sweetener in the top of a double boiler, set over simmering water, until pale yellow and thick, 3 to 5 minutes.

b) Add the Marsala and orange zest and continue cooking, whisking vigorously, until the mixture thickens enough to coat the back of a spoon.

c) Remove from the heat and stir in the Grand Marnier.

d) Divide among four dessert dishes. Serve warm or chilled. Top each serving with ¼ cup of whipped cream. Alternatively, chill the zabaglione and fold in the whipped cream, then divide among the dessert dishes.

65. Raspberries and cream

Ingredients:
- ½ cup heavy cream
- ¼ teaspoon vanilla extract
- 1 tablespoon sugar
- ½ packet aspartame sweetener
- 1 pint fresh raspberries

Directions:

a) Whip the cream with the vanilla, sugar, and aspartame until it forms soft peaks. Crush half the raspberries with a spoon and fold into the cream.

b) Divide the remaining berries among four dessert bowls and top with the raspberry cream. Cover and refrigerate until serving time.

66.   Fruit balls in bourbon

Ingredients:
- ½ cup melon balls
- ½ cup halved strawberries
- 1 tablespoon bourbon
- 1 tablespoon sugar
- ½ packet aspartame sweetener, or to taste
- Sprigs of fresh mint for garnish

Directions:

a) Combine the melon balls and strawberries in a glass dish.

b) Toss with the bourbon, sugar, and aspartame.

c) Cover and refrigerate until serving time. Spoon the fruit into dessert dishes and decorate with mint leaves.

67. Indian-style mangoes

Ingredients:
- 1 large ripe mango
- ½ lime
- ½ teaspoon curry powder

Directions:

a) Slice the mango in half lengthwise around the equator.

b) Twist between your hands to release the pit, which you'll discard.

c) Score the flesh of each half, making a fine crisscross pattern without cutting through the skin.

d) Turn each mango half inside out, and serve on a dessert plate sprinkled with lime juice and curry powder.

68. Italian cheesecake

Ingredients:
- 2 cups part-skim ricotta cheese
- 3 large eggs
- 2 tablespoons cornstarch
- 2 packets aspartame sweetener
- $1\frac{1}{2}$ teaspoons lemon extract
- 1 cup fresh raspberries
- $\frac{1}{4}$ cup all-fruit red currant preserves

Directions:

a) Preheat the oven to 325°F. Butter a 9-inch pie plate. In a large bowl, beat the ricotta and eggs together until smooth.

b) Beat in the cornstarch, sweetener, and lemon extract. Turn into the prepared pie plate. Bake on the middle shelf of the oven for 1 hour, or until a knife inserted in the center comes out clean.

c) Cool on a wire rack, then chill. Top with fresh raspberries. Melt preserves in a microwave on high (100 percent power) for 30 seconds, then drizzle over the berries.

d) Refrigerate until serving time.

69. Lemon fluff

Ingredients:
- 2 large eggs, separated
- 2 cups milk
- 1 envelope unflavored gelatin
- 1 packet aspartame sweetener
- 1 tablespoon sugar
- 2 teaspoons lemon extract
- 1 teaspoon grated lemon zest

Directions:

a) In a medium saucepan, beat the egg yolks until thick and lemony. Stir in the milk and gelatin and set aside for 5 minutes to soften.

b) Add the sweetener and sugar and cook over low heat, stirring constantly, for 5 minutes. Remove from the heat and stir in the lemon extract and zest.

c) Pour into a large, shallow bowl and chill in a large bowl filled with ice water.

d) Meanwhile, in a medium bowl, beat the egg whites until soft peaks form. Fold into the lemon mixture.

e) Spoon into six dessert dishes and chill until set.

70. Almond and coconut meringues

Ingredients:
- 3 large egg whites
- ¼ teaspoon kosher salt
- 3 packets aspartame sweetener
- 1 teaspoon almond extract
- ⅛ cup finely chopped almonds
- ½ cup shredded unsweetened coconut

Directions:

a) Preheat the oven to 250°F. In a squeaky-clean bowl, combine the egg whites, salt, and sweetener.

b) Beat with an electric mixer or whisk until the egg whites form stiff peaks. Fold in the almond extract, almonds, and coconut.

c) Drop by the heaping tablespoon onto a parchment paper-lined baking sheet.

d) Bake 30 minutes, then turn off the oven and allow the meringues to cool in the oven, without opening the door, at least 1 hour. Store in a tin.

71. Chocolate Chip Cookies

Servings: 12 cookies

Ingredients:

- ½ cup butter
- ⅓ cup cream cheese
- 1 egg beaten
- 1 teaspoon vanilla extract
- ⅓ cup erythritol
- ½ cup coconut flour
- ⅓ cup sugar-free chocolate chip

Directions:

a) Preheat the air fryer to 350°F. Line the air fryer basket with parchment paper and place the cookies inside

b) In a bowl mix butter and cream cheese. Add Erythritol and vanilla extract and whip up until fluffy. Add the egg and beat until incorporated. Mix in coconut flour and chocolate chips. Let the dough rest for 10 minutes.

c) Scoop out around 1 tablespoon of dough and form the cookies.

d) Place cookies in the air fryer basket and cook for 6 minutes.

72.   Air Fryer Brownies

yield: 2 SERVINGS

Ingredients:

- 1/3 cup Almond Flour
- 3 Tablespoons Powdered Sweetener
- 1/2 teaspoons Baking Powder
- 2 Tablespoons Unsweetened Cocoa Powder
- 1 Egg
- 4 Tablespoons Butter, melted
- 2 Tablespoons Chocolate Chips
- 2 Tablespoons Pecans, chopped

Directions:
a) Preheat the air fryer to 350 degrees.

b) In a mixing bowl, stir together the almond flour, baking powder, cocoa powder and powdered sweetener.

c) Add the egg and melted butter to the dry ingredients, and beat on high until smooth.

d) Stir in the pecans and chocolate chips.

e) Separate the batter into two separate well-greased ramekins.

f) Cook the cakes for 10 minutes as far from the heat source at the top of the air fryer as you can get them.

g) Let the brownies rest for 5 minutes before serving with your favorite toppings.

73. Berry Cheesecake

Yield: 8

Ingredients:

- 2 (8 oz.) blocks of cream cheese, softened
- 1 cup + 2 tablespoon confectioners' sweetener
- 2 eggs
- 1 teaspoon raspberry extract
- 1 cup berries

Directions:

a) In a large mixing bowl whip the cream cheese and Swerve sweetener until nice and creamy.

b) Add in the eggs and raspberry extract. Mix well.

c) In a blender or food processor, crush the berries and then mix into the cheesecake mixture along with the 2 extra tablespoons of Swerve.

d) Grease a spring-form pan and then spoon in the mixture.

e) Place pan into the basket of the air fryer and cook at 300°F for 10 minutes. Then lower the temperature to 250°F for 40 minutes. You know it's done when you gently shake the pan and everything seems set but the middle jiggles a little.

f) Take it out and let it cool down a bit before refrigerating. Keep it in the refrigerator for 24 hours. The longer the better to let it completely set up.

74. Donuts in the Air Fryer

Serves: 6

Ingredients:

- 1 ¼ cup almond flour 125 grams
- ⅓ cup granulated erythritol 60 grams
- 1 teaspoon baking powder
- ¼ teaspoon xanthan gum
- ⅛ teaspoon salt
- 2 eggs room temperature
- 2 tablespoons coconut oil melted
- 2 tablespoons unsweetened almond milk
- ½ teaspoon vanilla extract
- ¼ teaspoon liquid stevia
- Cinnamon Sugar Coating
- 4 tablespoons granulated erythritol
- 1 ½ teaspoons cinnamon

Directions:
a) In a large bowl, whisk together almond flour, erythritol, baking powder, xanthan gum, and salt.

b) In a medium bowl, lightly beat the room temperature eggs. Whisk in the melted coconut oil, almond milk, vanilla, and liquid stevia. Pour mixture into the bowl with dry ingredients and stir to combine.

c) Preheat air fryer at 330°F for 3 minutes. Spray donut pans or molds with avocado oil.

d) Pipe batter into six 3inch donut cavities, filling about 3/4 full. Tap pan on counter to settle batter and reduce air bubbles.

e) Bake donuts in air fryer at 330°F for 8 minutes. Check with toothpick for doneness. (With many air fryers, you may need to bake a set of 4 donuts first, then the remaining 2.)

f) Remove donuts from air fryer and let cool in pan for 5 minutes. Meanwhile, mix together the erythritol and cinnamon in a bowl (and bake the remaining donuts, if needed).

g) After cooling time, carefully remove donuts from pan and coat both sides of each donut with cinnamon sugar mix.

h) Place coated donuts in air fryer with the flatter side down. Bake at 350°F for 2 minutes, immediately coat with cinnamon sugar for a final time. Enjoy!

75. Vanilla Strawberry Cream Cake

Serves 6

Ingredients:

- 1 cup (100g) almond meal
- ½ cup (75g) Natvia
- 1 teaspoons (5g) baking powder
- 2 Tablespoons (40g) coconut oil
- 2 large eggs (51g each)
- 1 teaspoons (5g) vanilla extract
- 300ml cold cream
- 200g fresh ripe strawberries

Directions:
a) Preheat air fryer at 180°C, for 3 minutes.

b) In a large bowl, mix together almond meal, Natvia and baking powder with a pinch of sea salt.

c) Add coconut oil, eggs and vanilla and stir to combine.

d) Lightly brush a 16cm cake tin with extra coconut oil.

e) Using a spatula, scrape the mixture into the cake tin.

f) Pop in the air fryer basket and cover with a foil.

g) Cook at 160°C, for 20 minutes.

h) Remove foil and cook for another 10 minutes or until a skewer inserted removes clean.

i) When cool, whip the cold cream with an electric beater for 5 minutes or until stiff peaks form.

j) Spread across the cake and arrange the sliced strawberries on top.

k) Starting from the outside, use the larger slices (pointy side out) gradually working your way in.

l) Overlap each layer to create height.

76.   Berry Cobbler

Serves 4

Ingredients:

- 2 cups (250g) frozen blueberries, thawed
- ½ cup (120g) softened butter
- ¼ cup (38g) Natvia
- 2 eggs (51g each)
- ½ cup (50g) almond meal
- 1 teaspoons (5g) vanilla extract

Directions:
a) Preheat air fryer at 180°C, for 3 minutes.

b) Place the thawed blueberries into the base of an 8 x 8cm ceramic dish or loaf tin.

c) In a bowl, mix together remaining ingredients with a pinch of sea salt and spoon over blueberries.

d) Poke gently to mix slightly the berries and almond mixture.

e) Place the dish in the air fryer.

f) Cover with foil.

g) Bake at 180°C, for 10 minutes. Remove foil and bake for another 5 minutes or until well browned.

77. Chocolate Bundt Cake

Serves 6

Ingredients:

- 1 ½ cups (150g) almond meal
- ½ cup (75g) Natvia
- ⅓ cup (30g) unsweetened cocoa powder
- 1 teaspoons (5g) baking powder
- ⅓ cup (85g) unsweetened almond milk
- 2 large eggs (51g each)
- 1 teaspoons (5g) vanilla extract

Directions:
a) Preheat air fryer at 180°C, for 3 minutes.

b) In a large mixing bowl, stir all ingredients until well combined.

c) Spray a mini Bundt tin with oil. NB: Bundt cake tins come in a variety of sizes, the size that you need will depend on the size of your air fryer. A light spray with oil, or brush with melted butter will prevent sticking.

d) Scoop the batter into the tin.

e) Place in the air fryer basket and cook at 160°C, for 10 minutes.

f) Cool for 5 minutes before removing.

78. Giant PB Cookie

Serves 4

Ingredients:

- ⅓cup (33g) almond meal
- 2 Tablespoons (24g) Natvia
- 1 large egg (51g)
- 3 Tablespoons (75g) crunchy peanut butter
- 1 teaspoons (3g) cinnamon

Directions:

a) Preheat air fryer at 180°C, for 3 minutes.

b) Place all ingredients in a bowl with a pinch of sea salt and mix to combine.

c) Spoon the mixture onto a round of baking paper and lightly push to spread, keeping the thickness of the mixture as even as possible.

d) Cook at 180°C, for 8 minutes.

79. Dessert Bagels

Makes 4

Ingredients:

- 1 cup (100g) almond meal
- ½ teaspoons (2.3g) baking powder
- ¼ cup (75g) shredded mozzarella
- 1 Tablespoons (20g) cream cheese
- 1 large egg (51g)

Directions:

a) Preheat air fryer at 180°C, for 3 minutes.

b) Mix the almond meal and baking powder together. Season with a pinch of salt.

c) Melt the mozzarella and cream cheese in a bowl in the microwave for 30 seconds.

d) Cool, then add the egg. Stir to combine.

e) Add the almond meal and knead into a dough.

f) Divide into 4 even portions, roll into sausages, 8cm long.

g) Pinch the ends together to make a donut shape.

h) Place on baking paper.

i) Bake at 160°C, for 10 minutes.

80. Bread Pudding

Serves: 2

Ingredients
- Nonstick spray, for greasing ramekins
- 2 slices of white bread, crumbled
- 4 tablespoons of white sugar
- 5 large eggs
- ½ cup cream
- Salt, pinch
- 1/3 teaspoon of cinnamon powder

Directions
a) Take a bowl and whisk eggs in it.
b) Add sugar and salt to the egg and whisk it all well.
c) Then add cream and use a hand beater to incorporate the entire ingredients.
d) Now add cinnamon, and add crumbs of bread.
e) Mix it well and add into a round shaped baking pan.
f) Put it inside the air fryer.
g) Set it on AIRFRY mode at 350 degrees F for 8-12 minutes.
h) Once it's cooked, serve.

81. Mini Strawberry and Cream Pies

Serves: 2

Ingredients
- 1 box Store-Bought Pie Dough, Trader Joe's
- 1 cup strawberries, cubed
- 3 tablespoons of cream, heavy
- 2 tablespoons of almonds
- 1 egg white, for brushing

Directions:
a) Take the store brought pie dough and flatten it on a surface.
b) Use a round cutter to cut it into 3-inch circles.
c) Brush the dough with egg white all around the parameters.
d) Now add almonds, strawberries, and cream in a very little amount in the center of the dough, and top it with another circular.
e) Press the edges with the fork to seal it.
f) Make a slit in the middle of the dough and put it into the basket.
g) Set it to AIR FRY mode 360 degrees for 10 minutes.
h) Once done, serve.

82.   Brazilian Grilled Pineapple

Servings: 4

Ingredients

- 1 pineapple, peeled, cored and cut into spears
- 1/2 cup (110 g) Brown Sugar
- 2 teaspoons (2 teaspoons) Ground Cinnamon
- 3 tablespoons (3 tablespoons) melted butter

Directions:

a) In a small bowl, mix together brown sugar and cinnamon.

b) Brush the pineapple spears with the melted butter. Sprinkle cinnamon sugar over the spears, pressing lightly to ensure it adheres well.

c) Place the spears into the air fryer basket in a single layer. Depending on the size of your air fryer, you may have to do this in batches.

d) Set fryer to 400°F for 10 minutes for the first batch (6-8 minutes for the next batch as your air fryer will be preheated). Halfway through, brush with any remaining butter.

e) Pineapples are done when they are heated through and the sugar is bubbling.

83. Coconut Crusted Cinnamon Bananas

Ingredients
- 4 ripe, but firm Bananas
- ½ cup of Tapioca Flour
- 2 large Eggs
- 1 cup of Shredded Coconut Flakes
- 1 heaped teaspoon of Ground Cinnamon
- Coconut spray

Directions:
a) Cut each banana into thirds

b) Make an assembly line:

c) Pour the tapioca flour into a shallow dish.

d) Crack the eggs in another shallow bowl and whisk lightly.

e) Combine the shredded coconut and the ground cinnamon in the third shallow dish. Mix well.

f) Dredge the bananas in tapioca flour and shake off the excess.

g) Dip the bananas in the beaten eggs. Make sure it is completely coated in egg wash.

h) Roll the bananas in the cinnamon-coconut flakes to fully coat it. Press it firmly to make sure the coconut flakes are adhering to the bananas. Keep them in a flat tray.

i) Liberally spray the Air Fryer basket with coconut oil.

j) Arrange the coconut crusted bananas pieces in the fryer basket. Spray with more coconut spray.

k) Air fry at 270F for 12 minutes.

l) Dust with ground cinnamon and serve warm or at room temperature with a scoop of ice-cream.

84. Gluten Free Easy Coconut Pie

Yield: 6-8

Ingredients
- 2 eggs
- 1 1/2 cups milk
- 1/4 cup butter
- 1 1/2 teaspoons vanilla extract
- 1 cup shredded coconut
- 1/2 cup Monk Fruit
- 1/2 cup coconut flour

Directions:

a) Coat a 6" pie plate with non-stick spray and fill it with the batter. Continue following the same instructions as above.

b) Cook in the Air Fryer at 350 degrees for 10 to 12 minutes.

c) Check the pie halfway through the cooking time to be sure it is not burning, give the plate a turn, use a toothpick to test for doneness.

85. Pecan Pudding

Ingredients:
- 1 tablespoon Butter or Margarine
- 1 Large Beaten Egg White
- 1/3 cup Dark Corn Syrup
- 1/4 teaspoon Vanilla
- 2 tablespoon Unbleached Flour
- 1/8 teaspoon Baking Powder
- 1/4 cup Chopped Pecans
- Powdered Sugar

Directions:

a) In a 15-ounce custard cup microwave the butter or margarine, uncovered, on 100% power for 30 to 40 seconds or just till melted.
b) Swirl the butter in the custard cup, coating sides and bottom.
c) Pour the excess butter from the custard cup into the beaten egg.
d) Stir in the dark corn syrup and vanilla.
e) Stir together flour and baking powder.
f) Stir flour mixture into egg mixture. Gently fold in chopped pecans.
g) Pour the pecan mixture into the buttered 15-ounce custard cup. Microwave, uncovered, on 50% power for 3 to 4 minutes or till the pecan mixture is just set, rotating the custard cup a half-turn every minute.
h) Sift a little powdered sugar atop. Serve warm with light cream, if desired.

86.   Coffee Liqueur Mousse

Ingredients:
- 4 eggs, separated
- 1/4 c coffee liqueur
- 1/4 c maple syrup
- 1/8 c cognac
- 1 c water
- 1 c whipping cream

Directions:

a) In a blender or with electric beater, blend together egg yolks, maple syrup and water. Transfer to a saucepan and bring to a boil. Remove from heat and add coffee liqueur and cognac. Chill.
b) Beat cream and egg whites until soft peaks form.
c) Carefully fold into chilled liqueur mixture.
d) Spoon into demitasse glasses, and chill 2 hours.

87.   Peach Melba Dessert

Ingredients:
- 2 c Peaches; sliced, peeled
- 2 c Raspberries
- 3/4 c Sugar
- 2 tablespoons Water
- Ice cream; vanilla

Directions:

a) In a saucepan, bring peaches, raspberries, sugar, and water to a boil.
b) Reduce heat and simmer 5 minutes.
c) Chill, if desired.
d) Serve over ice cream.

88. Frozen Cinnamon Nut Yogurt

Ingredients:
- 4 c Vanilla yogurt
- 1 c Sugar
- 1/2 teaspoons Cinnamon
- Salt
- 1 c Whipping cream
- 1 teaspoons Vanilla
- 1 c Walnut pieces

Directions:

a) Thoroughly combine yogurt, sugar, cinnamon and salt in mixing bowl. Stir in whipping cream and vanilla. Add nuts.
b) Cover and refrigerate 30 minutes.
c) Freeze according to manufacturer's directions.

89.   Five-minute fudge

Ingredients:

- 2/3 cup Evaporated Milk
- 1-2/3 cup Sugar
- 1/2 teaspoon Salt
- 1-1/2 cup Marshmallows (Miniatures work best)
- 1-1/2 cup Chocolate Chips (Semi-sweet)
- 1 teaspoon Vanilla

Directions:

a) Combine Milk, Sugar and Salt in saucepan over medium heat.
b) Bring to a boil and cook 4-5 minutes, stirring constantly (start timing when the mixture starts to "bubble" around the corners of the pan). Remove from heat. Add Marshmallows, Chocolate Chips and vanilla. Stir vigorously for 1 minute (or until Marshmallows are completely melted and blended). Pour into a buttered 8" square pan. Cool until it doesn't fall out or slosh around in pan.
c) You like nuts? Add 1/2 cup chopped nuts before pouring in pan.

90. Almond-Oat Crust

Ingredients:
- 1 c. ground almonds
- 1 c. oat flour
- 1/2 teaspoon salt
- 1/4 c. water or juice

Directions:

a) GRIND almonds and oats in blender until fine, or grind oats and almonds in food processor, adding salt and water while processor is in motion. ADD salt, mixing well. ADD water. MIX well. PRESS into pie pan, or roll out with rolling pin between two pieces of wax paper.

b) BAKE at 350° for 15 minutes. YIELD: 1 pie crust.

91.   Apple Fantasy Dessert

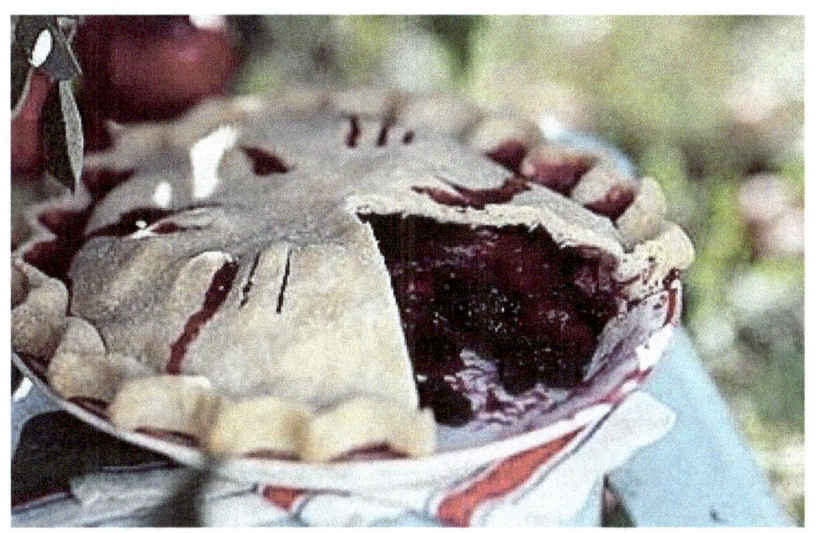

Ingredients:
- 2/3 c. flour
- 3 teaspoon baking powder
- 1/2 teaspoon salt
- 2 eggs
- 1 c. granulated sugar
- 1/2 c. brown sugar
- 3 teaspoon vanilla or rum or bourbon
- 3 c. diced apples

Directions:

a) Beat eggs, add sugar and vanilla and beat well. Add dry ingredients and mix. Dump in apples and stir until evenly distributed. Put in a deep baking dish or soufflé dish.
b) Bake 45 minutes at 350. Serve warm.

92. Avocado ice cream

Ingredients:
- avocados
- lemon juice
- 1 can (14 oz. / 400ml) full-fat coconut milk
- 1 cup / 100g preferred liquid sweetener such as maple syrup or agave syrup

Directions:

a) Place the can of coconut milk in the fridge overnight.
b) Cut the avocados in half, remove the pit and spoon out the avocado flesh.
c) Put the avocado flesh in a food processor together with the lemon juice and blend until it's a perfectly smooth avocado cream.
d) Open the coconut milk can upside down (so that the hard cream is on top).
e) Spoon out the coconut cream until you hit the coconut water
f) Whip the coconut cream in a bowl until it's a nice, soft coconut whipped cream. Add in the avocado cream and the rice syrup and mix until incorporated.
g) Put the ice cream in a freezer-safe dish.
h) Place it in the freezer for at least 4 hours.
i) If it is too hard to spoon out after 4 hours, let it sit at room temperature for a minute or two. Enjoy!

93. Banana Cream Pie

Ingredients:
- 3 c. SOY MILK (58)
- 1/2 c. honey
- 1/2 c. raw cashews
- 1/4 teaspoon salt
- 1/3 c. cornstarch
- 2 teaspoon vanilla
- 1/3 c. pitted dates
- 2-3 sliced bananas

Directions:

a) LIQUEFY all ingredients except bananas. POUR into a saucepan, and cook over medium heat until thickened, stirring constantly. POUR a thin layer of the "custard" mixture into a baked pie shell or layer of granola, then ADD a layer of sliced bananas.

b) Repeat, then add the remaining custard, and garnish with sliced almonds. CHILL overnight, and SERVE cold.

94. Berry Fool

Ingredients

- 1 (12-ounce) package frozen raspberries or strawberries (not in syrup), thawed
- 1/4 cup plus 1 tablespoon sugar, divided
- 1 cup heavy whipping cream

Directions

a) In a blender or food processor, combine raspberries or strawberries with 1/4 cup sugar. Process until berries are pureed, scraping down sides when necessary.

b) In a large bowl, beat heavy cream with mixer until soft peaks form. Add remaining 1 table-spoon sugar and continue whipping until stiff peaks form.

c) Using a rubber spatula, gently fold in the raspberry puree, leaving some streaks of white whipping cream. Spoon into four individual parfait glasses. Refrigerate for 2 hours then serve.

95. Berry tiramisu

Ingredients

- 1 1/2 cups brewed coffee
- 2 tablespoons Sambuca
- 1 tablespoon granulated sugar
- 1-pound container mascarpone cheese
- 1/4 cup heavy cream
- 2 tablespoons confectioners' sugar
- Ladyfinger cookies
- Cocoa powder
- 2 cups mixed berries

Directions

a) In a shallow bowl, whisk together 1 1/2 cups brewed coffee, 2 tablespoons Sambuca and 1 tablespoon granulated sugar until the sugar is dissolved.

b) In a separate bowl, whisk together one 1-pound container mascarpone cheese, 1/4 cup heavy cream and 2 tablespoons confectioners' sugar.

c) Using enough ladyfinger cookies to cover the bottom of an 8-inch square baking dish, dip the ladyfingers in the coffee mixture and arrange in an even layer at the bottom of the pan.

d) Spread half of the mascarpone mixture on top. Repeat the two layers. Sprinkle with cocoa powder and 2 cups mixed berries. Refrigerate the tiramisu for at least 2 hours and up to 2 days.

96. Butter Rum Caramels

Ingredients
- Vegetable oil for greasing
- 2 cups packed light brown sugar (14 oz.)
- 1 cup heavy cream
- 1/2 stick (1/4 cup) unsalted butter
- 1/4 teaspoon salt
- 1/4 cup plus 1 teaspoon dark rum
- 1/4 teaspoon vanilla
- Special equipment: parchment paper; a candy or deep-fat thermometer

Directions:

a) Line bottom and sides of an 8-inch square baking pan with parchment paper and oil parchment.

b) Bring brown sugar, cream, butter, salt, and 1/4 cup rum to a boil in a 3- to 4-quart heavy saucepan, stirring until butter is melted, then boil over moderate heat, stirring frequently, until thermometer registers 248°F (firm-ball stage), about 15 minutes. Remove from heat and stir in vanilla and remaining teaspoon rum. Pour into baking pan and cool completely until firm, 1 to 2 hours.

c) Invert caramel onto a cutting board, then discard parchment and turn caramel glossy side up. Cut into 1-inch squares.

97. Candied Citrus Peel

Ingredients:
- zest of 4 lemons, 3 oranges, or 2 grapefruits
- 1 cup sugar
- 1/3 cup water

Directions

a) First simmer zest in 1-quart water for 6 min. Drain, rinse with cold water, and set aside. Bring sugar and water to simmer.
b) When sugar dissolves, cover pan and boil a few minutes until last drops of syrup fall from the end of a metal spoon to form a thread. Remove from heat, stir in peel, and steep 1 hr.
c) Ready to use or store covered in refrigerator.

98. Cardamom-Coconut Panna Cotta

Ingredients
- 1 cup unsweetened coconut flakes
- 3 cups heavy cream
- 1 cup buttermilk
- 4 green cardamom pods, lightly crushed Pinch kosher salt
- 2 teaspoons granulated gelatin
- 1 tablespoon water
- ⅓ cup granulated sugar
- teaspoon rose water

Directions

a) Preheat the oven to 350°. Scatter the coconut on a sheet pan and place in the oven. Bake until toasted and golden, about 5 minutes. Remove from the oven and set aside.

b) In a medium saucepan set over medium-high heat, combine the heavy cream, buttermilk, cardamom and salt and bring just to a boil. Remove the pan from the heat, add the toasted coconut and set aside for 1 hour. Strain the mixture through a fine-mesh sieve and discard the solids.

c) In a medium bowl, combine the gelatin and water. Set aside for 5 minutes.

d) In the meantime, return the saucepan to medium heat, add the sugar and cook until the sugar dissolves, about 1 minute. Carefully pour the strained cream mixture over the gelatin mixture and whisk until the gelatin dissolves. Whisk in the rose water and divide the mixture into 8 four-ounce ramekins. Place in the refrigerator and chill until firm, at least 2 hours up to overnight

e) Make the candied rose petals: Line a baking sheet with parchment paper. In a small bowl, combine the sugar and cardamom. Use a pastry brush to brush both sides of each rose petal with the egg white and carefully dip in the sugar. Set aside to dry completely on the parchment paper

f) Serve the panna cotta chilled and garnish each serving with rose petals.

99.   Chicory cream brulee

Ingredients:
- 1 tablespoon butter
- 3 cups heavy cream
- 1 1/2 cups sugar
- 1 cup Chicory coffee
- 8 egg yolks
- 1 cup raw sugar
- 20 small shortbread cookies

Directions

a) Preheat the oven to 275 degrees F. Grease 10 (4-ounce) ramekins. In a saucepan, over medium heat, combine the cream, sugar and coffee.

b) Whisk until smooth. In a small mixing bowl, whisk the eggs until smooth. Temper the egg yolks into the hot cream mixture. Remove from the heat and cool. Ladle into the individual ramekins. Place the ramekins in a baking dish.

c) Fill the dish with water coming up half of the ramekin. Place in the oven, on the bottom rack and cook until the center is set, about 45 minutes to 1 hour.

d) Remove from the oven and water. Cool completely.

e) Refrigerate until chilled. Sprinkle the sugar over the top, shaking off the excess. Using a hand-blow torch, caramelized the sugar on top. Serve the cream brulee with shortbread cookies.

100. Mint Chocolate Fondue

Ingredients:
- 1/2 cup Heavy Cream
- 2 tablespoons Peppermint Liqueur
- 8 ounces Semisweet Chocolate

Directions
a) Warm the heavy cream over medium low heat
b) Add liqueur
c) Grate the chocolate or break into small pieces and slowly add to mixture while stirring
d) Stir until the chocolate is melted

CONCLUSION

Protein and fat are fundamental macro-nutrients that back all vital structures in your body. Digging out the perfect dessert from the store shelf is a challenge. You cannot easily find a Dessert that is nutritional and wholesome at the same time while containing your favorite ingredients.

If you are a fan of these decadent goodies but are scared of feeding yourself preservatives and excessive sugar, then this cookbook is your guilt-free recourse. With a selection from protein packed recipes to fat-loaded recipes, you will never get bored with these.

www.ingramcontent.com/pod-product-compliance
Lightning Source LLC
Chambersburg PA
CBHW070657120526
44590CB00013BA/991